Ups and Downs, Grins and Frowns

Learning to Obey out of Love for God

Authorized by the Wisconsin Evangelical Lutheran Synod

Northwestern Publishing House
Milwaukee, Wisconsin

STRONG Roots FOR *tender* Shoots

Sometimes we can walk just fine
And never trip or stumble.

But other times we take steps
That make us fall and tumble.

Our lives are very much like that.
Sometimes we do what's right.

But other times we don't obey.
We say bad things or fight.

Jesus wants us to obey
To show our love for him.

When we don't follow his commands,
We disobey; we sin—

Tripping, hitting, biting,
Or pulling someone's hair;

Talking mean or fighting
Or saying, "I won't share!"

Jesus says these things are wrong.
So do not push or shove.

Don't wear a face that's mean and long
And hasn't any love.

But gladly do what grown-ups say,
And ask, "Can I help you?"

Show love for others every day.
Be kind and helpful too.

Remember, Jesus died for you to take your sins away.

Show love for him in all you do.
He loves you every day!

Be Kind

Lynn Groth

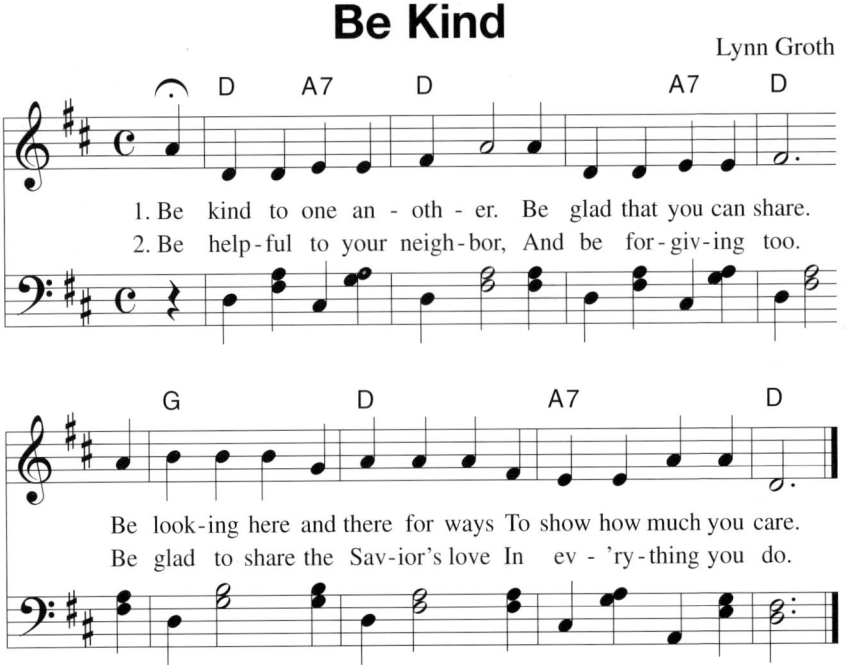

The song above and the rhyming verses below can be used together as a simple play.

    Sing stanza 1 of the song. Speak verse 1.
    Sing stanza 1 again. Speak verse 2.
    Close by singing stanza 2 of the song.

1. **May I help you with your coat?** *(pretend to hold coat)*
   Please, let me get the door. *(pretend to open door)*
   I can share my snack with you. *(pretend to open sack)*
   Still hungry? Have some more!

2. **Here! You dropped your crayon.** *(pretend to pick up crayon)*
   Let's rake our neighbor's yard. *(pretend to rake)*
   Let's help people sad or sick.
   Let's make a get-well card! *(hold hands together like card; open; close)*

You may wish to use a real coat, snack, crayon, rake, and card to act out the verses.

Text, Tune, Setting: © 1997 Northwestern Publishing House.